A TRANSITIONAL METHOD

AS its name implies, the present work is a transitional method, especially designed for those individuals desirous of affecting a transfer from one instrument to another. The important role played by the viola in orchestral and chamber music literature, as well as its ever increasing popularity as a solo instrument, certainly is justification for *all* violinists becoming thoroughly acquainted with the intricacies of the larger instrument. A close relationship exists between the violin and the viola, but because of this it is not to be assumed that they are played in an identical fashion. In reality, each instrument has peculiarities common only to itself.

VIOLA BOWING — When studying viola, violinists should give their immediate attention to the production of a tone characteristic of the instrument. The melancholy, contralto voice of the viola, so different from that of the violin, does not depend entirely upon the instrument itself; rather it depends to a great extent upon the manner in which the instrument is bowed. To develop bowing technic so necessary for the production of a tone worthy of the viola, players must draw the bow with the hair absolutely flat upon the string. A constant effort should be made to produce as large a tone as possible, but the tone at all times should be *drawn* from the instrument and not forced from it. Furthermore, players should avoid using the extreme tip of the bow, and when changing from down bow to up bow, and vice versa, they should play in a detaché style, i.e., avoid stopping the tone. Exceptions to this are to be found only in the playing of spiccato and staccato bowings.

VIOLA FINGERING — Viola notation, which is established by the alto clef, is quite easy for violinists to read. An expedient for violinists acquainted with the third position of their instrument, is to disregard the alto clef entirely, and assume that they are reading notation established by the treble clef with the addition of two flats to the signature. It immediately will be seen that the fingering of the viola in the first position is identical with that of the violin in the third position.

INTONATION — Intonation on the violin and viola is relatively the same; yet due to a wider spacing of the fingers in the production of whole-steps on the viola, violinists transferring to that instrument sometimes find it difficult to play in tune. Half-steps on the two instruments are played alike, i.e., with consecutive fingers touching each other. Strict observance of this fact on the viola, coupled with the testing of fourth finger tones against open strings, and the regular practice of simple octaves, played both melodically and harmonically, will aid materially in establishing a true intonation on the larger instrument.

"C" STRING RESONANCE — The production of a resonant tone on the "C" string of the viola should be given paramount attention by all violinists transferring to that instrument. The use of large violas has been advocated as a means of securing this resonance, but only too often large instruments as well as small instruments possess an unresponsive, dull-sounding "C" string. The regular practice of sustained tones, crescendos, and crescendo-diminuendos on the "C" string will do considerable toward developing resonance on the lower string of the viola.

FINGER STRENGTH — Finger strength, so essential for violinists transferring to the viola, will not develop entirely with its own accord; rather it must be acquired through the regular practice of specific exercises in which individual fingers are raised as high as possible and then struck with all possible force upon the fingerboard while other fingers remain securely in place.

POSITION STUDY — Although the present volume is confined to the first position of the viola, it is quite necessary for all students of the instrument to be acquainted with the existing higher positions, as well as the half-position, which so frequently is used in orchestral literature. To accomplish this end, players should turn, upon completion of this work, to the pages of *Introducing the Positions* for Viola, Volume One, and begin at once the all-important study of the higher positions of the instrument.

HARVEY S. WHISTLER, Ph.D.

Stringing and Tuning the Viola

VIOLA *(Italian)*   BRATSCHE *(German)*   QUINTE *(French)*

MANNER OF STRINGING THE VIOLIN

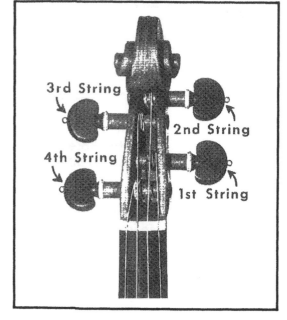

MANNER OF STRINGING THE VIOLA

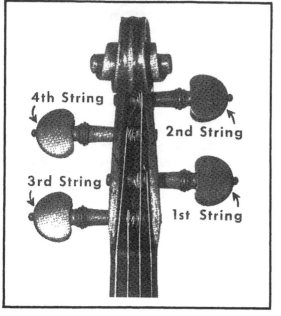

The stringing of the violin and viola differs. The third and fourth strings of the viola are strung in a manner opposite that of the corresponding strings of the violin. The purpose of this reversed stringing on the left hand pegs of the viola is to avoid the abrupt "bend" that comes to the thick fourth string of that instrument if strung in violin style.

Violin music is written in notation of the treble clef with "Middle C" on the first line below the staff.

The Violin is tuned in fifths.

Viola music is written chiefly in notation of the alto clef, with "Middle C" on the third line of the staff.

The Viola is tuned in fifths, but a fifth lower than the violin.

VIOLIN OPEN STRINGS   VIOLA OPEN STRINGS

Viola Notation and Fingering
(First Position)

Transitional Studies
(For Daily Practice)

Viola Bowing

To produce a characteristic viola tone, draw the bow with the hair flat, parallel to the bridge, half way between the bridge and fingerboard. Play with as large a tone as possible. but "draw" the tone from the instrument rather than force it. Avoid using the extreme tip of the bow. When changing from down bow to up bow, and vice versa, avoid stopping the tone unless playing a staccato type of bowing.

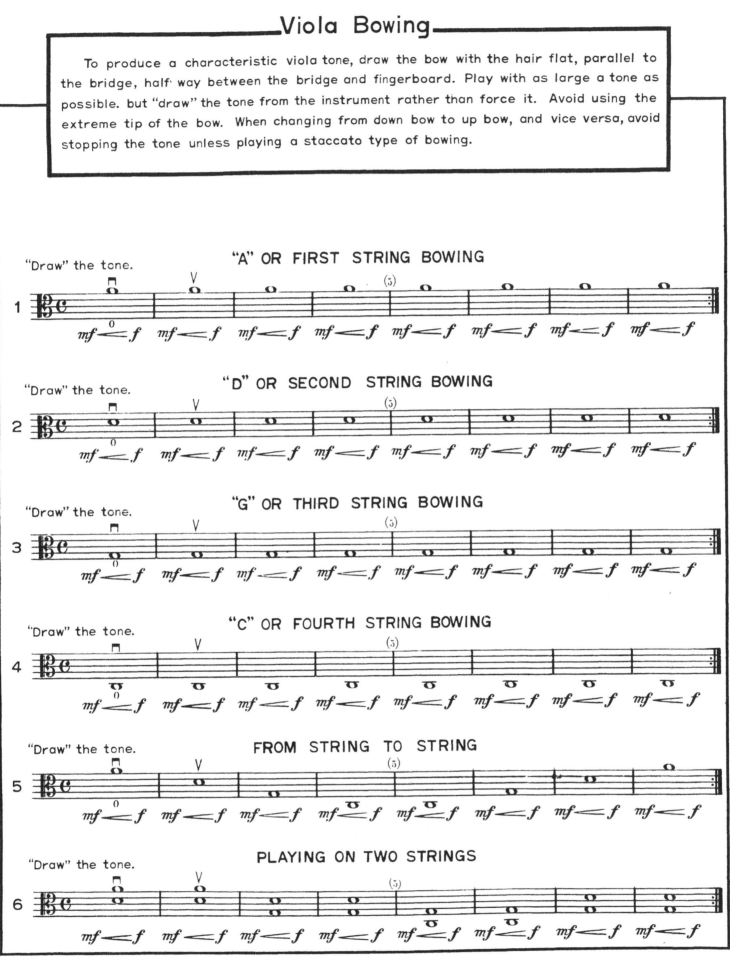

Transitional Studies *(Cont'd)*
(For Daily Practice)

Viola Fingering

An expedient for players acquainted with the third position of the violin, which will result in an immediate reading of viola notation, is to disregard the alto clef entirely and assume that they are reading notation established by the treble clef with the addition of two flats to the signature. It immediately will be seen that the fingering of the viola in the first position is identical with the fingering of the violin in the third position.

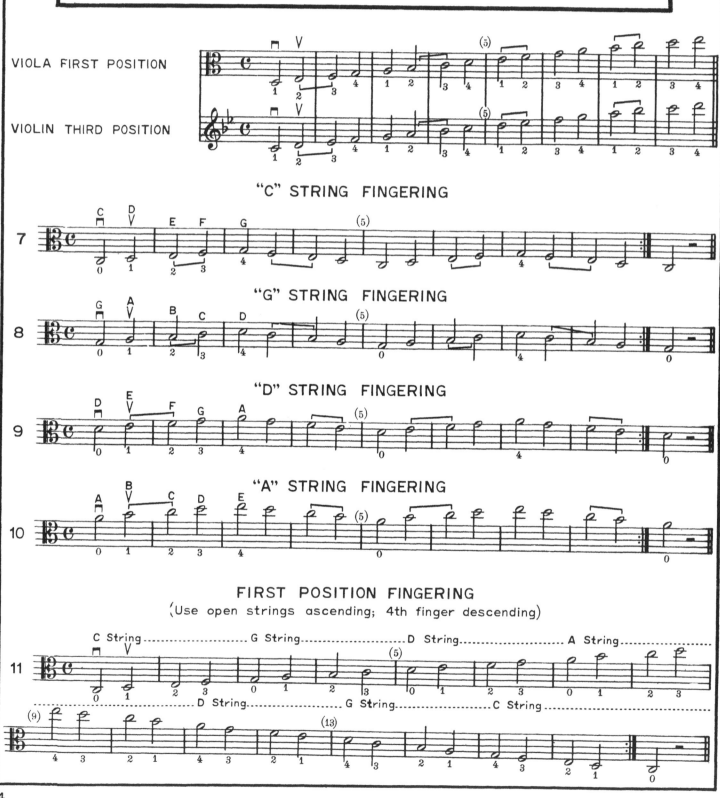

Transitional Studies *(Cont'd)*
(For Daily Practice)

Intonation

Intonation on the viola is relatively the same as on the violin; yet due to a wider spacing of the fingers in the production of whole-steps, students transferring from the latter instrument to the former find it difficult to play in tune. It must be noted that half-steps are close together, and fingers producing the same must touch each other. The exercises given below, with half-steps marked, fourth fingers tested against open strings, and octaves played melodically and harmonically, when practiced regularly, will aid materially in establishing a true intonation on the viola.

Transitional Studies *(Cont'd)*
(For Daily Practice)
"C" String Resonance

The production of a resonant tone on the "C" string of the viola is a matter of great concern to all players of that instrument. The exercises given below will aid materially in solving this problem, but must be practiced with the hair of the bow in a flat position on the string as the tone is "drawn" from the instrument.

CRESCENDO

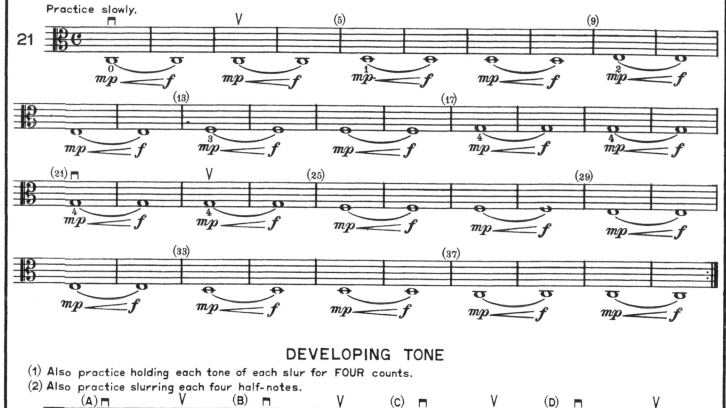

DEVELOPING TONE

(1) Also practice holding each tone of each slur for FOUR counts.
(2) Also practice slurring each four half-notes.

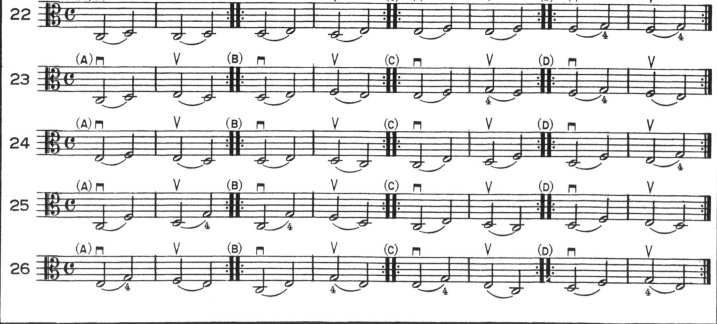

Transitional Studies *(Cont'd)*
(For Daily Practice)
Finger Strength

Finger strength is a requisite of all viola players. This strength will not develop with its own accord, but rather must be acquired through certain practice procedures. The exercises given below, which were devised by the famous Polish virtuoso, Henri Wieniawski, will aid materially in developing finger strength, but must be practiced at a slow tempo, with the finger producing the upper tone in each instance raised as high as possible and then struck with all possible force on the fingerboard. Fingers not actively engaged in producing the tones indicated must be held down at all times.

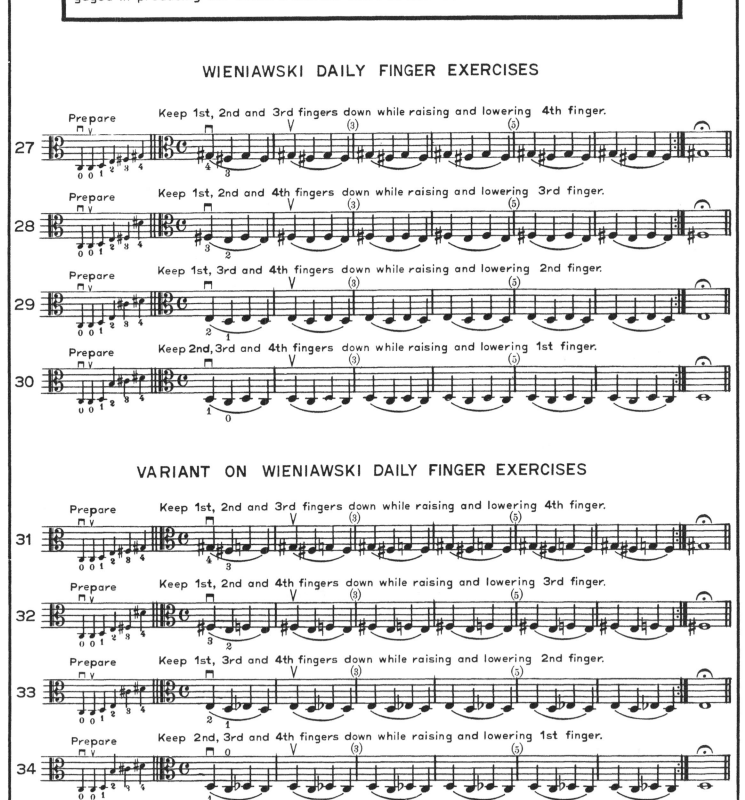

WIENIAWSKI DAILY FINGER EXERCISES

VARIANT ON WIENIAWSKI DAILY FINGER EXERCISES

Key of C Major

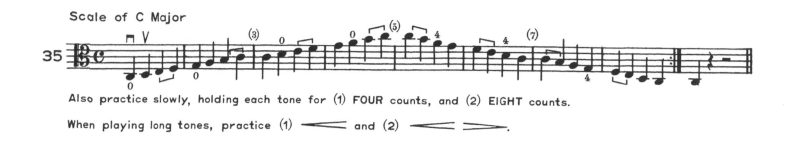

Also practice slowly, holding each tone for (1) FOUR counts, and (2) EIGHT counts.

When playing long tones, practice (1) ⟨ and (2) ⟨ ⟩.

Etude in C

BRUNI

Also practice slurring each four tones.

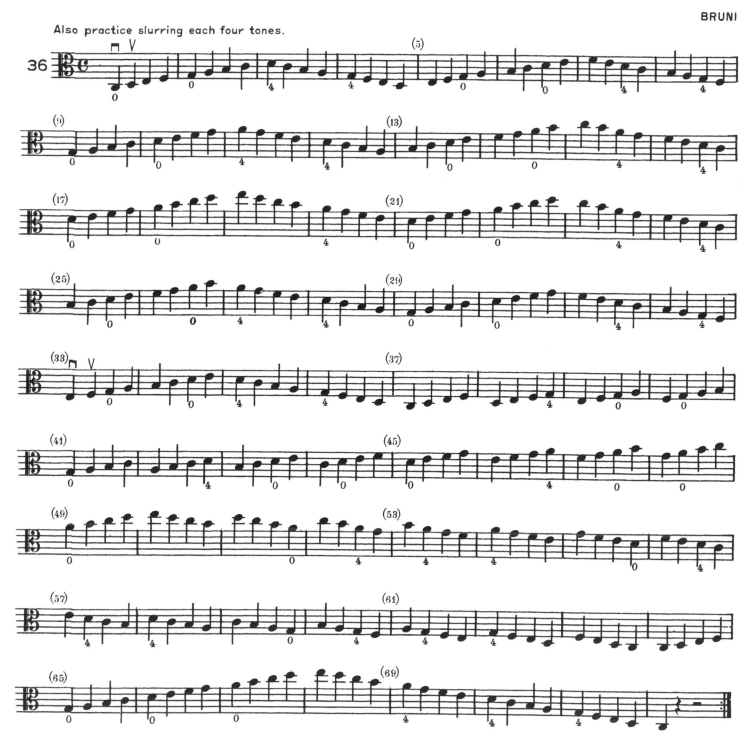

MELODIC THIRDS

RITTER

FROM STRING TO STRING

CAMPAGNOLI

CHROMATIC SCALE FROM "C"

SPOHR

SLURRED THIRDS

CAMPAGNOLI

Swiss Air
(Duet)

MAZAS

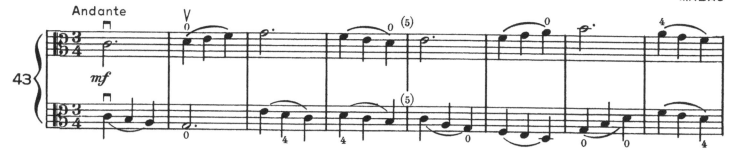

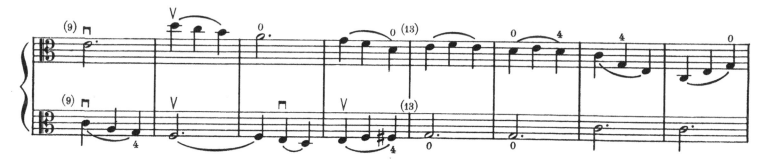

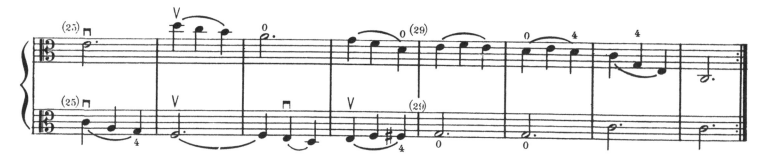

SLURRED SIXTHS

CAMPAGNOLI

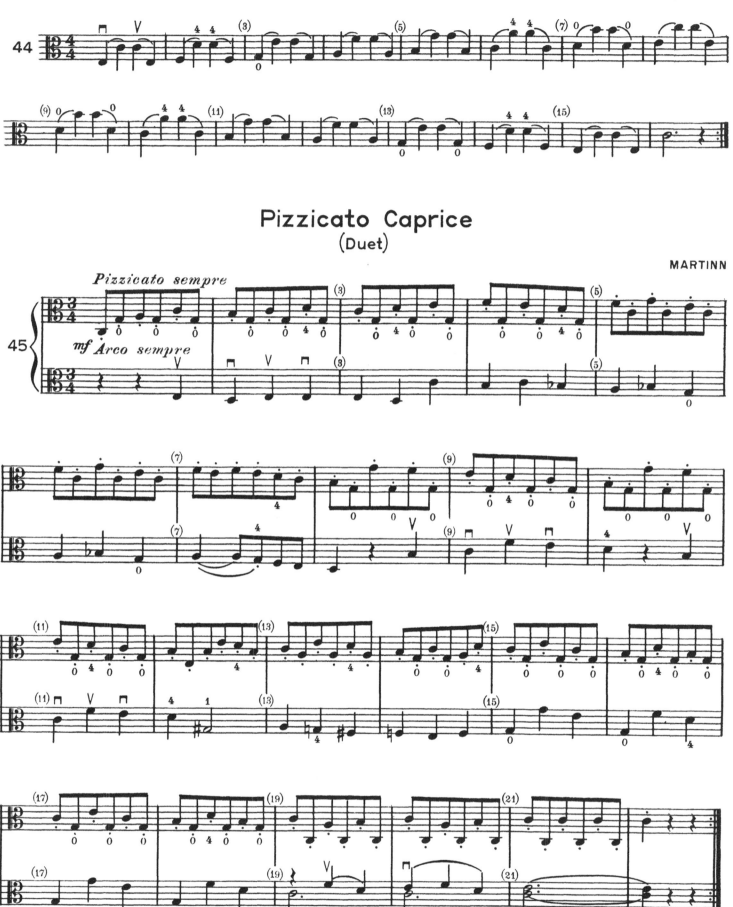

Pizzicato Caprice
(Duet)

MARTINN

11

Key of G Major

Scale of G Major

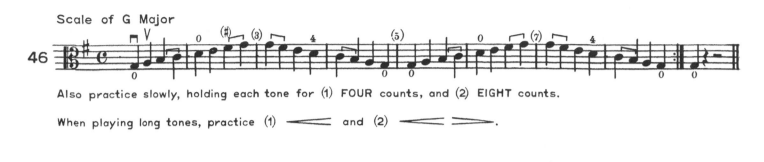

Also practice slowly, holding each tone for (1) FOUR counts, and (2) EIGHT counts.

When playing long tones, practice (1) ⟨ and (2) ⟨⟩ .

Etude in G

GRÜNWALD

Also practice slurring each four tones.

CHROMATIC SCALE FROM "G"

SPOHR

Air and Variation

MAZAS

Moderato
(AIR)

(VARIATION)

(AIR)

* $\widehat{4}$ = Fourth finger extended.

Pastorale

SITT

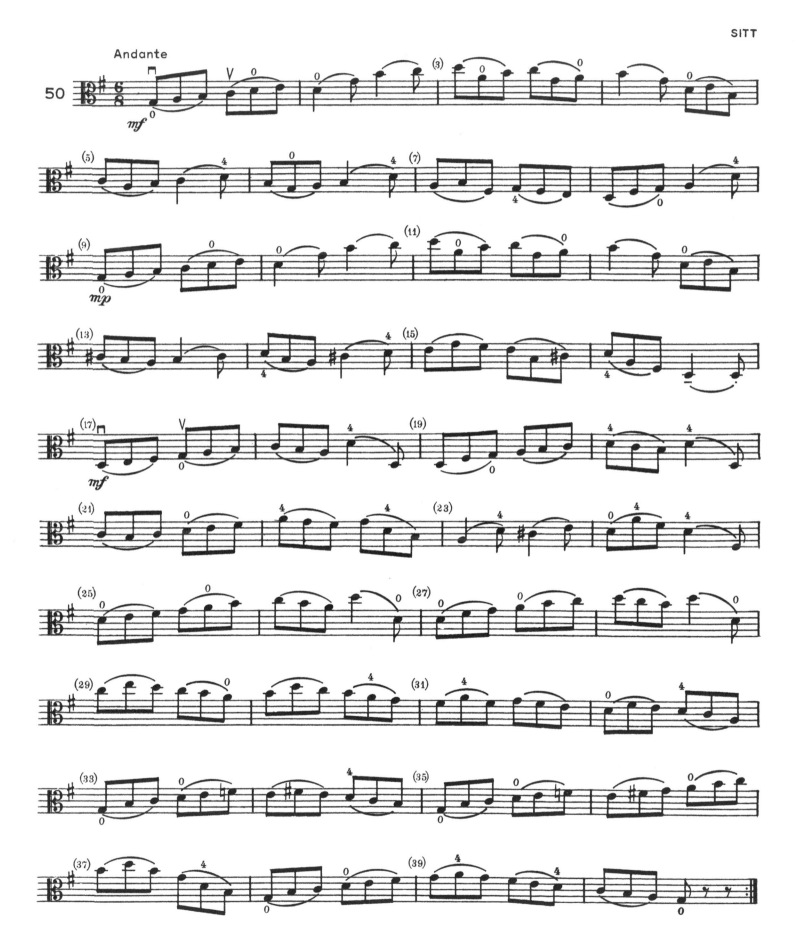

Hungarian Rondo

HAYDN

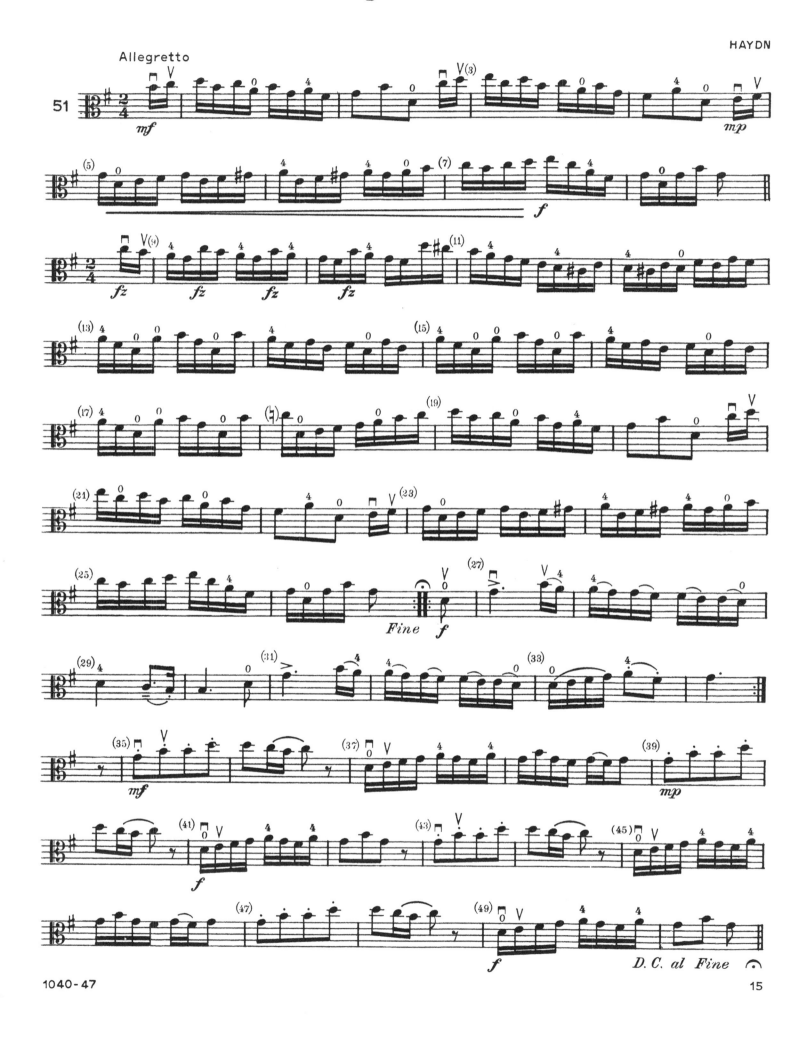

Key of F Major

Scale of F Major

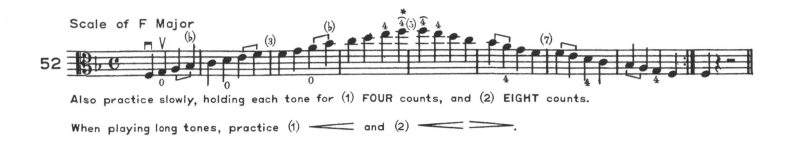

Also practice slowly, holding each tone for (1) FOUR counts, and (2) EIGHT counts.

When playing long tones, practice (1) ◁‾‾‾ and (2) ◁‾‾‾▷.

Etude in F

WICHTL

Also practice slurring each four tones.

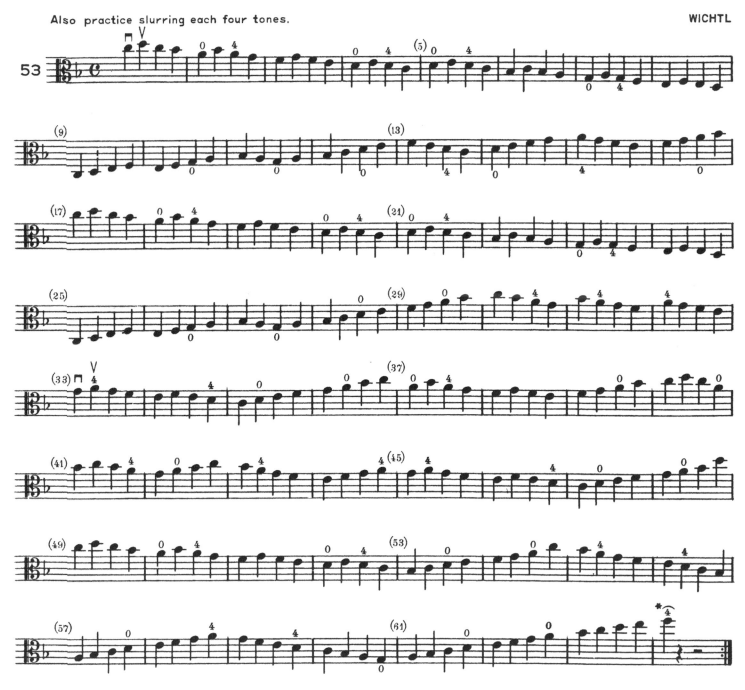

* $\widehat{4}$ = Fourth finger extended.

Finger Extension

CAMPAGNOLI

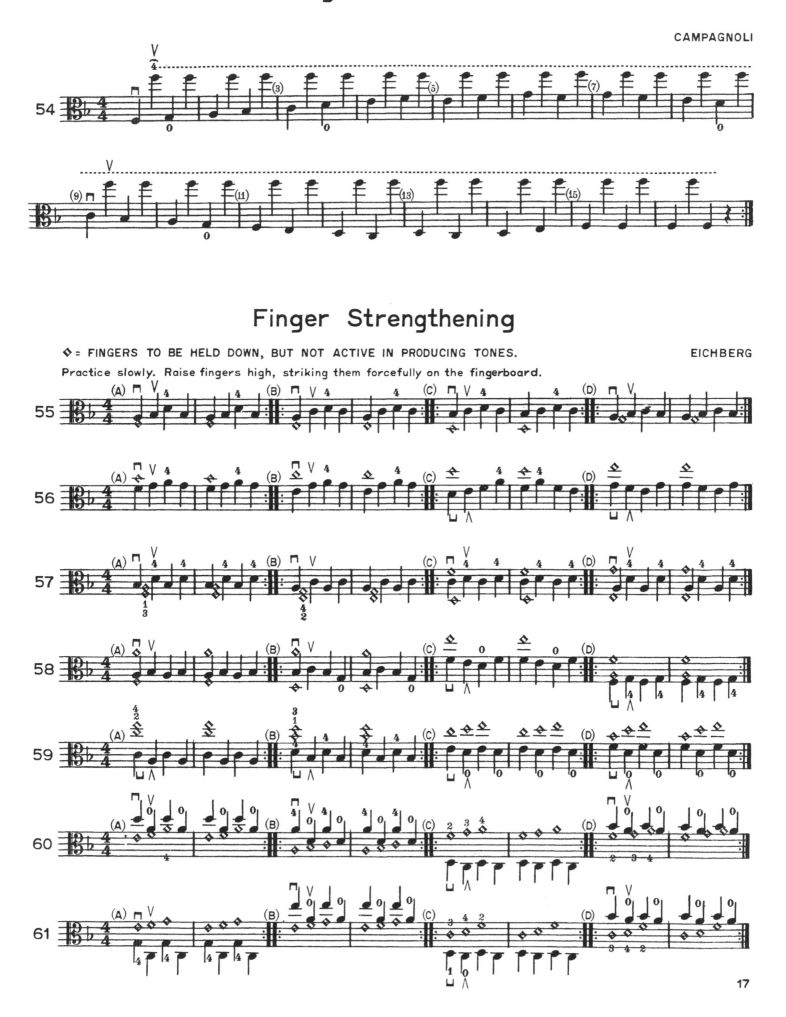

Finger Strengthening

◊ = FINGERS TO BE HELD DOWN, BUT NOT ACTIVE IN PRODUCING TONES.

EICHBERG

Practice slowly. Raise fingers high, striking them forcefully on the fingerboard.

Double-Stops

When playing double-stops on the viola, draw the bow with the hair flat, slightly nearer the bridge than the fingerboard. Play with as large a tone as possible, but "draw" the tone from the instrument, rather than force it. The fingers of the left hand must be held securely in place, once the correct pitch has been established.

ALARD

18

Three-Note Chords

When playing three-note chords on the viola, draw the bow with the hair flat, slightly nearer the bridge than the fingerboard. First play the lower and middle tones together, immediately tilting the bow, and playing the middle and upper tones together. Gradually, the tones of three-note chords on the viola may be played simultaneously.

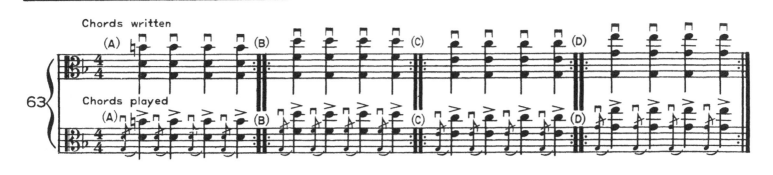

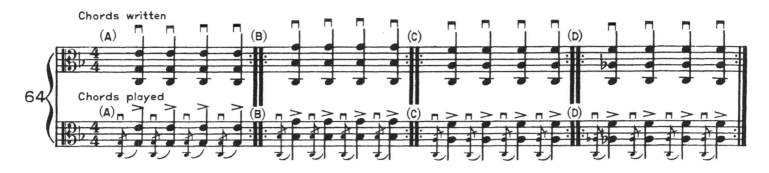

Four-Note Chords

When playing four-note chords on the viola, draw the bow with the hair flat, slightly nearer the bridge than the fingerboard. First, play the lower two tones together, immediately tilting the bow and playing the upper two tones together.

Key of D Major

Scale of D Major

67

Also practice slowly, holding each tone for (1) FOUR counts, and (2) EIGHT counts.

When playing long tones, practice (1) ◁————▷ and (2) ◁————▷————◁.

Etude in D

KAYSER

Also practice using a separate bow for each tone.

68

Praeludium

SCHUMANN

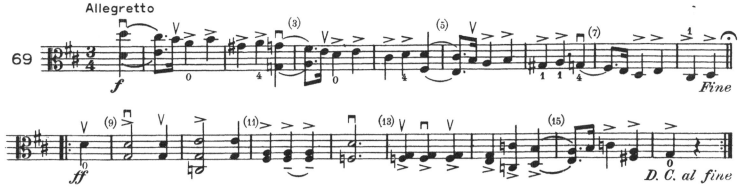

Allegretto

69

Fine

D. C. al fine

Tanz

DAVID

Allegro ben moderato (spiccato)

70

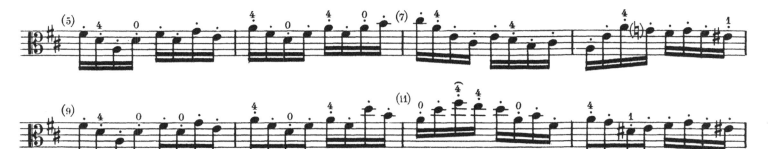

* $\widehat{4}$: Fourth finger extended.

CHROMATIC SCALE FROM "D"

SPOHR

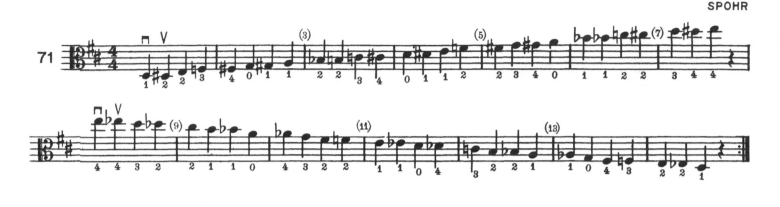

Syncopation Study

SITT

Tempo giusto

Menuet

D. C. al Fine
(senza replica)

Key of B♭ Major

Scale of B♭ Major

Also practice slowly, holding each tone for (1) FOUR counts, and (2) EIGHT counts.

When playing long tones, practice (1) ◁— and (2) ◁——▷.

Etude in B♭

HOFMANN

Also practice using a separate bow for each tone.

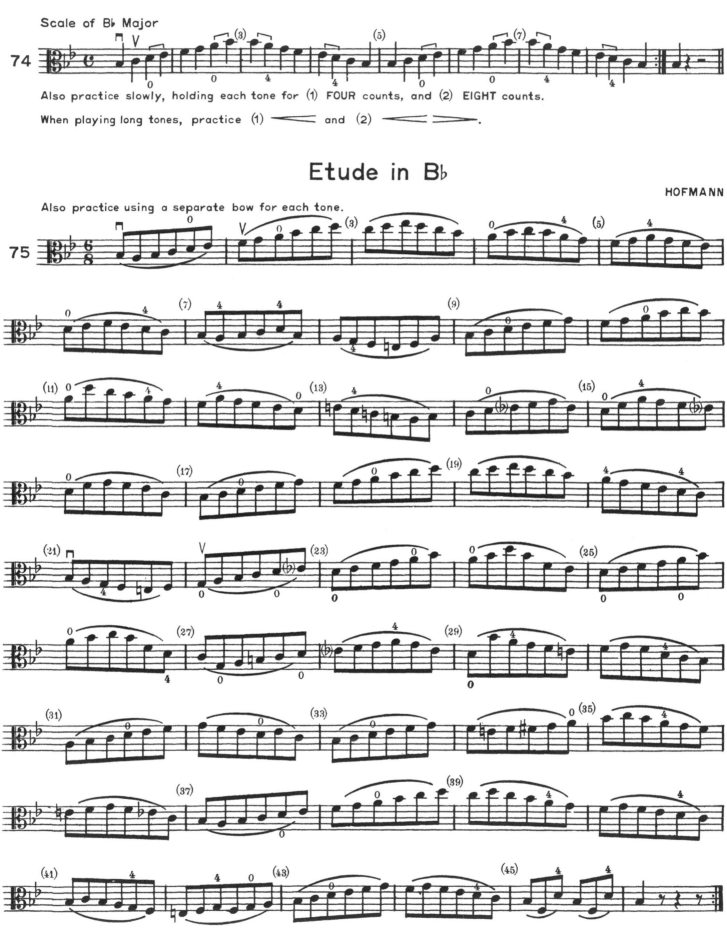

Danse Allemande

BEETHOVEN

Caprice Symphonic

HOFMANN

Chromatic Fantasy

SPOHR

27

Key of A Major

Scale of A Major

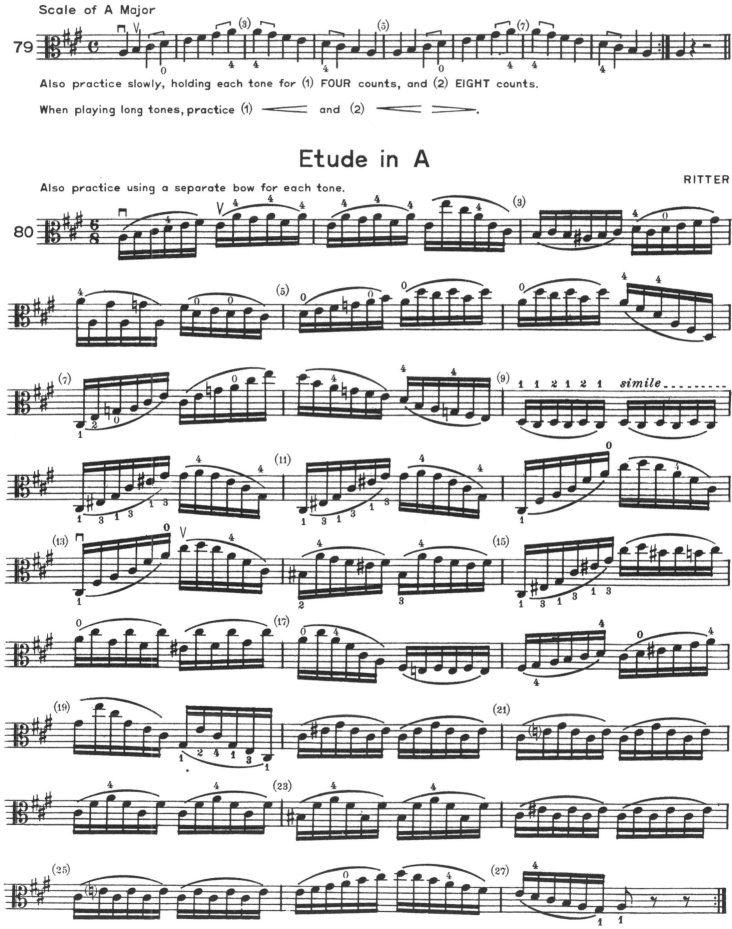

Also practice slowly, holding each tone for (1) FOUR counts, and (2) EIGHT counts.

When playing long tones, practice (1) ⟨ and (2) ⟨⟩.

Etude in A

RITTER

Also practice using a separate bow for each tone.

In Forest and Meadow
(Duet)

BAVARIAN AIR

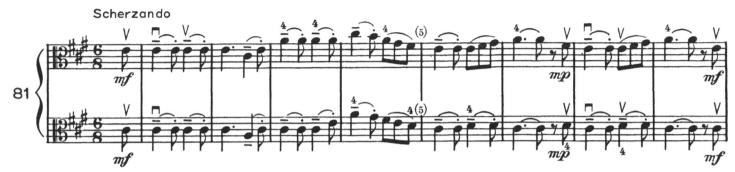

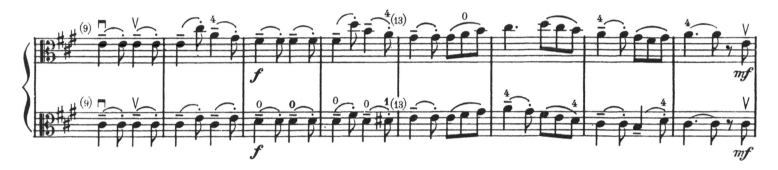

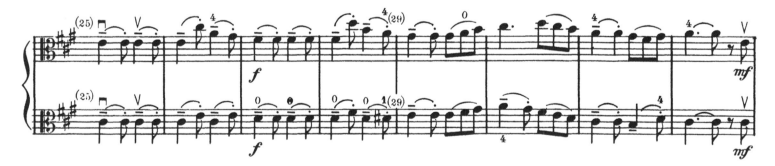

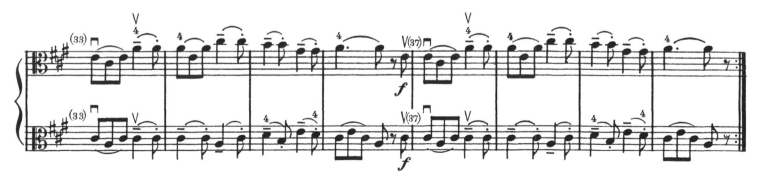

Romance
from Symphony No. 18

HAYDN

Finale from Lustspiel Overture
(Orchestral Excerpt)

KÉLER BÉLA

Key of E♭ Major

Scale of E♭ Major

84

Also practice slowly, holding each tone for (1) FOUR counts, and (2) EIGHT counts.

When playing long tones, practice (1) ◁◁ and (2) ◁▷.

Etude in E♭

Also practice slurring each two tones.

KAYSER

85

* 4̂ = Fourth finger extended.

Eventide

SITT

If I Were King
(Orchestral Excerpt)

ADAM

Allegretto
(Change of Key)

Allegro

Bowing Study

KAYSER

Bowings to be practiced:

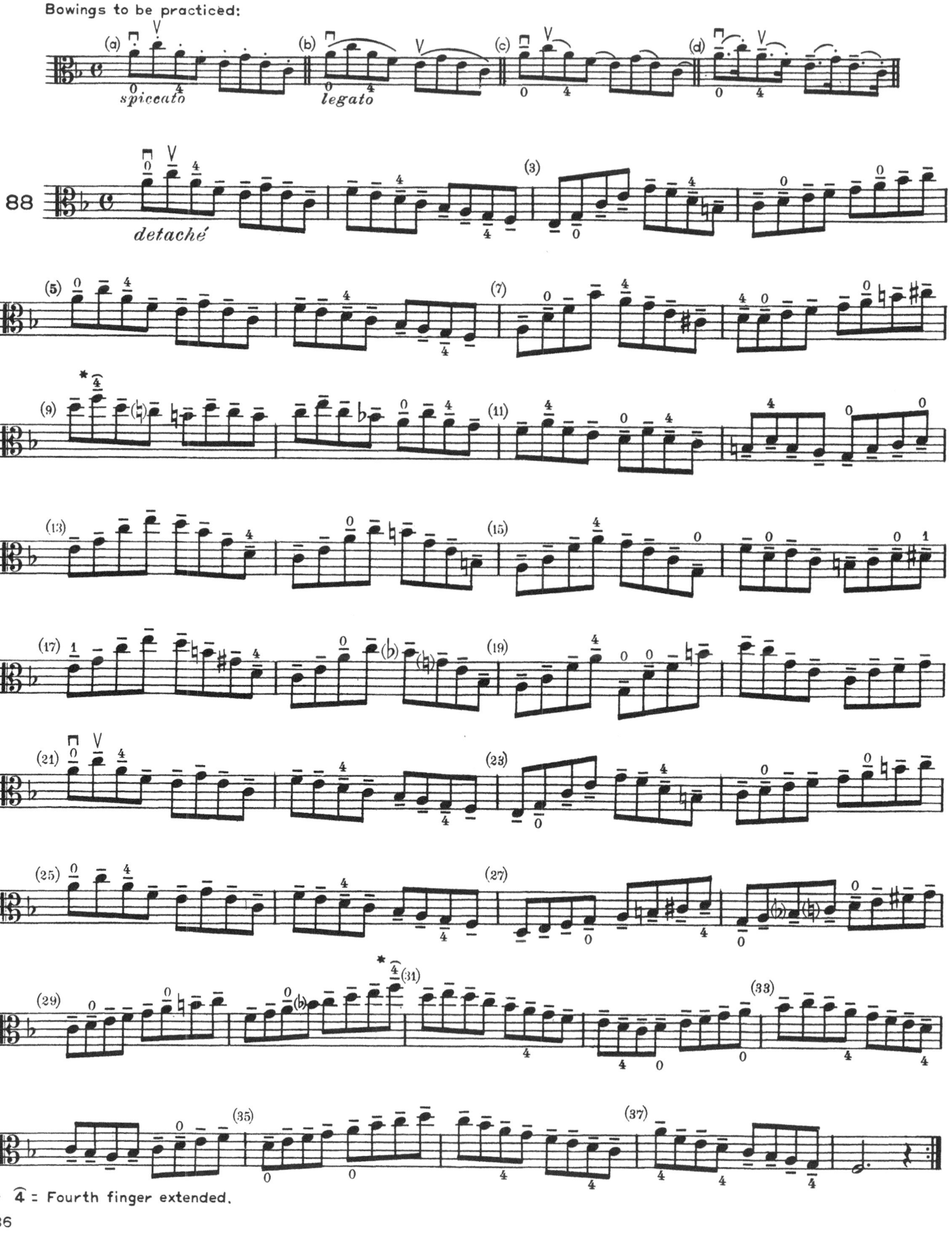

spiccato

legato

88 detaché

* $\widehat{4}$ = Fourth finger extended.

36

Advanced Intonation Studies

SCHRADIECK

Also practice very slowly, using a separate bow for each tone.

* $\widehat{4}$ = Fourth finger extended.

Advanced Studies for "C" String Resonance

CRESCENDO

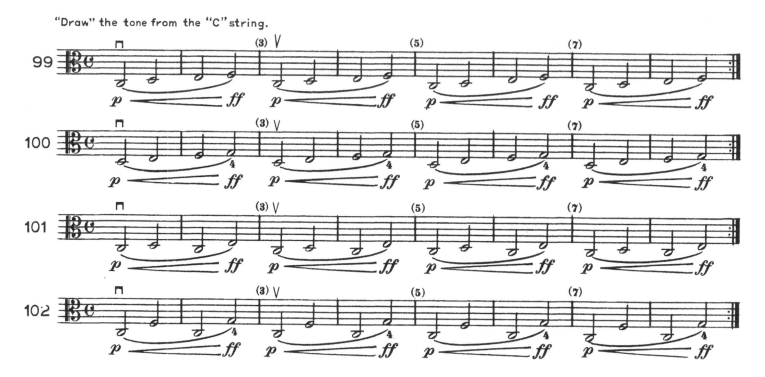

CRESCENDO - DIMINUENDO

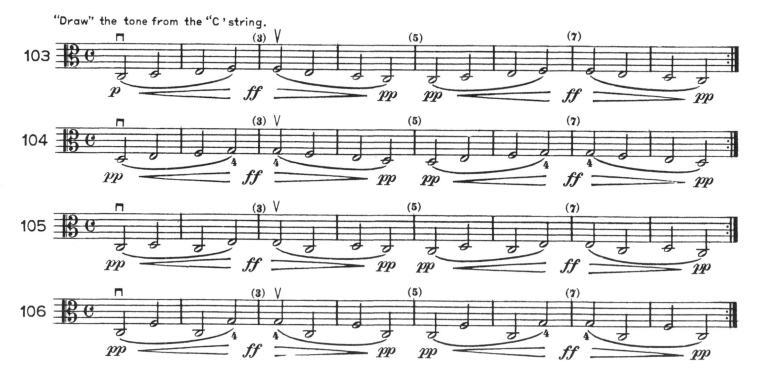

SOSTENUTO

Key of A Minor

Scherzo-Caprice

RIES

Leggiero

* $\widehat{4}$ = Fourth finger extended.

Key of E Minor

Scale of E Harmonic Minor

110

Scale of E Melodic Minor

111

Also practice slowly, holding each tone for (1) FOUR counts, and (2) EIGHT counts.

When playing long tones, practice (1) ⟨— and (2) ⟨—⟩.

Tarantella

SARASATE

Vivace

112

Key of D Minor

Scale of D Harmonic Minor

113

Scale of D Melodic Minor

114

Also practice slowly, holding each tone for (1) FOUR counts, and (2) EIGHT counts.

When playing long tones, practice (1) ⟨ and (2) ⟨ ⟩.

Theme and Variation
from the 24th Caprice

PAGANINI

Allegro
(THEME)

115

(VARIATION)

Key of B Minor

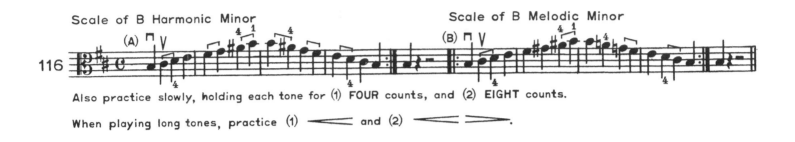

Scale of B Harmonic Minor   Scale of B Melodic Minor

116

Also practice slowly, holding each tone for (1) FOUR counts, and (2) EIGHT counts.

When playing long tones, practice (1) ——=◁ and (2) ◁=——=◁.

Cortége

RIES

Maestoso

117

Key of G Minor

Scale of G Harmonic Minor   Scale of G Melodic Minor

118
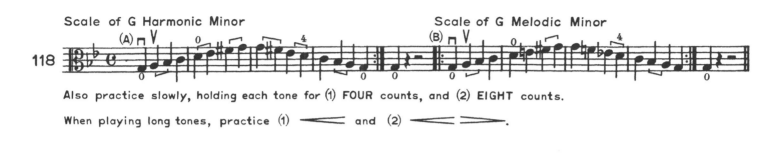

Also practice slowly, holding each tone for (1) FOUR counts, and (2) EIGHT counts.

When playing long tones, practice (1) ‾‾◁ and (2) ‾◁▷‾.

Danse Norse
from the Northern Suite

GADE

Allegro

119

Key of F# Minor

Scale of F# Harmonic Minor

120

Scale of F# Melodic Minor

121

Also practice slowly, holding each tone for (1) FOUR counts, and (2) EIGHT counts.

When playing long tones, practice (1) ——— and (2) ———.

Matinee

MAZAS

Moderato

122

* $\widehat{4}$ = Fourth finger extended.

44

Key of C Minor

Scale of C Harmonic Minor

123

Scale of C Melodic Minor

124

Also practice slowly, holding each tone for (1) FOUR counts, and (2) EIGHT counts.

When playing long tones, practice (1) ⬍ and (2) ⬍.

Intermezzo
from the First String Quartet

MENDELSSOHN

Allegretto

125

p *leggiero sempre*

Loure

BACH

* $\widehat{4}$ = Fourth finger extended.

Folies d' Espagne
(Theme with Variations)

CORELLI

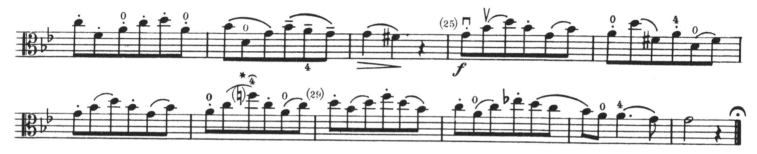

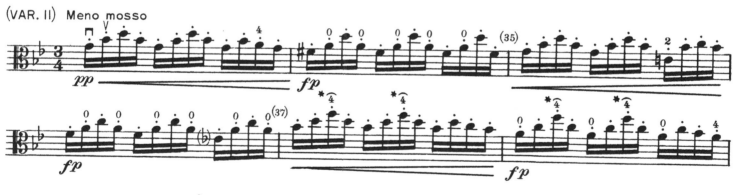

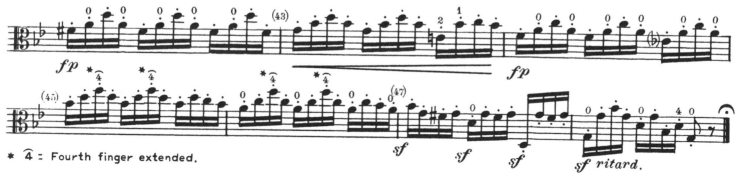

* $\widehat{4}$ = Fourth finger extended.

Etude d' Artiste

RITTER

For the continuation of this course of study, turn to "Introducing the Positions for Viola," Volume I, by Harvey S. Whistler, and commence the study of the third position on the Viola.

48